HOW

ANYONE

SAY

GOD

IS

GOOD

ISBN: 978-1-943929-98-6

Cover and interior layout design: Kristi Yoder

Second printing: January 2018

Published by:
TGS International
P.O. Box 355, Berlin, Ohio 44610 USA
Phone: 330-893-4828
Fax: 330-893-2305
www.tgsinternational.com

TGS001613

HOW CAN ANYONE SAY

GOD IS GOOD

GARY MILLER

NICK'S BACK ACHED as he hauled his bike up the stairway of the apartment building. At least this way he knew it wouldn't disappear. He frowned, remembering the one he had lost. He wasn't taking any more chances with locks and chains. As he wrestled the bike around the landing and up the final set of stairs, he heaved a sigh. Unlocking the door and leaning the bike against the entry wall, he headed for the kitchen, grabbed a beer from the fridge, and stumbled into the living room, where he flopped into a recliner.

What a miserable day! Everything had gone wrong. The boss had chewed him out for being late. Then Tim hadn't shown up, so Nick had to walk his route too, delivering mail in the cold drizzle of an early fall day.

But that was nothing compared to the quarrel

with Jessica. He glanced at the clock on the stereo. In half an hour his girlfriend would get home from work. How was he going to face her? He knew he'd really blown it. How could he piece things back together?

When Jessica had moved in two years ago, things had been great. They had gone out together every weekend. Her companionship had filled a lonely spot in Nick's life. But lately something had changed, and tensions in their relationship had been mounting. Nick rubbed his forehead, struggling to put his finger on what it was. Jessica seemed distant and irritable the last few weeks. He recalled the way she had snapped at him for leaving his boots lying in the doorway. Sure, he had his faults, but he had tried hard to make her happy. He thought of the times he had bought pizza for her when she didn't feel like cooking, the movies he had watched because they were interesting to her. But somehow things had still turned sour. What had gone wrong?

Finally last night things had come to a head. He had been drinking too much, and his pent-up frustration had boiled over. Even now he cringed, remembering the cutting words he had shouted at

Jessica. He knew he had hurt her deeply. Never, until this morning, had he seen her unwilling to talk. Now, what could he do to make it up to her?

Nick sighed, staring blankly out the window. He had hoped for a different kind of home than this. A home like the one he had known as a child, before his parents divorced, when life had a sense of normalcy and predictability. Those had been happy times. Christmas with everyone together, family vacations . . .

What he wouldn't give to have that kind of family life again! Maybe he could patch things up with Jessica. After all, they had often talked and dreamed of having children and enjoying the rest of their lives together. Maybe he could apologize and buy her some fresh flowers.

Having settled on a course of action, Nick leaned back into the recliner to finish his beer. But his anxiety refused to be quieted. What if Jessica still wouldn't talk?

He pushed the troublesome thought aside. It was easier to reminisce about the past than to face the present. He thought again of his childhood home—a fairly traditional, even old-fashioned, family arrangement. With just one sister and a dad who made enough money to provide for their needs, he'd had nothing to complain about. His mother attended church every Sunday, and even though his dad stayed home and watched television, he agreed with his wife that the children needed religion. So every Sunday Nick and his sister trailed along behind their mother to church. Now, years later, he could still remember some of the songs and verses they had learned in Sunday school.

He could also remember his doubts. Even as a boy, he had wondered—if religion was so important, why didn't Dad need it? Nick had harbored a secret suspicion that Jesus was for wimps and women.

Then when Nick was just twelve years old, his cozy little world had suddenly imploded.

Nick and his sister had come home from school one afternoon to find their house locked. No one was home. Their mother had disappeared. Unknown to the family, she had been involved with a man from her church, and now her note informed them that she had run off to "start a new life." A life that didn't include Nick or his sister.

Although many years had passed, Nick could

still taste the agony of that night. He could picture himself burrowed under the covers, sobbing himself to sleep. For the next few weeks he had existed in a haze of misery and confusion. Finally the numbness of being betrayed by his mother had given way to bitter resentment.

He had learned some things back then. First, that everything Mom had told him about a loving god was a lie. She had taught him to pray, encouraged him to memorize verses from the Bible, and insisted that he go to church. She had claimed to have this wonderful "personal relationship with God," whatever that meant. And yet she had turned around and abandoned her family! Since then Nick hadn't believed in God. Even if there was a god, it certainly wasn't the one Mom worshiped!

Nick had never felt close to his dad, not even after his mom left. To cover up his loneliness, he had poured his time and energy into school. He had always loved computers, and for the next several years he pursued this passion. He graduated from college with a degree in computer science. He smiled as he remembered how proud he'd been to receive his diploma. But his grin faded as he recalled how he had submitted job application after job application with no luck. Still, he had faced the future with optimism. He had taken a job with the postal service, confident that he would eventually find the high-paying career of his dreams. In the meantime he had decided to get all the fun out of life that he could.

That was three years ago, Nick realized with slight surprise. He flipped up the footrest of the recliner. *Why aren't things working out as I had planned?* He frowned.

Shrugging off his doubts, he turned back to the problem at hand. How could he appease Jessica? She would be home soon, and he knew her well enough to know this wasn't going to be easy. Heading to the kitchen for another beer, he suddenly thought of Eric, his closest friend. Of course! Why hadn't he thought of him before? He'd always been able to trust Eric's advice. Surely he would have some good ideas. The thought of his buddy brought a grin to Nick's face. He reached for his phone. With Eric's help he could find a solution before Jessica got home.

Then he saw the note.

It was in plain sight on the kitchen counter, but

in his anxiety he had overlooked it. He snatched it up and read the hastily scrawled message.

Nick,

I lay in bed last night thinking back over our time together and the things you said. I concluded that I have been a fool to stay with you this long, so I am leaving. I am taking the money we had been saving for future plans. If you don't think that's fair, then think about who paid for the furniture you're sitting on. This seems about even to me. Don't forget, the rent was due last week.

Since you'll find out soon enough anyway, I'll just tell you now. Eric and I have been involved in a relationship for the last couple of months, and he has been trying to get me to move in with him. I wasn't sure that was what I wanted . . . till last night.

—Jessica

CHAPTER TWO

THE INSISTENT ALARM finally penetrated his dreamy fog. With a groan Nick rolled over, his fingers searching for the button that silenced the unwelcome intrusion. *There!* Nick slumped back against the soft mattress, his head throbbing, trying to bring his thoughts into focus. *I really should get out of bed before Jessica has to remind me.* Subconsciously he had been waiting for her insistent elbow. He squinted over the crumpled pillow. Was she already up?

Then the memory of last night's shock hit him like a sickening wave. He'd lost Jessica. And his best friend Eric.

Nick stumbled from the bedroom, grabbing the doorway for support. With bleary eyes he surveyed the chaotic living room. It looked like a war zone. Pieces of paper and pizza crusts littered the floor, a chair was knocked over, and beer cans were scattered on every horizontal surface. Nick rubbed his forehead. *I wonder how I made it safely to the bedroom.* Despondently he kicked a couple of cans out of his path and aimed for the recliner. Falling into its welcoming softness, he laid his head back, closed his eyes, and tried to ignore the relentless headache and nausea of a massive hangover.

He squinted at the clock. If he didn't get moving, he'd be late for work again. But he didn't even care. As his mind regained alertness, all the pain he had briefly escaped last night came crashing back. Never before had life seemed so dark.

Nick had experienced disappointment before. When his mother had left, he thought he would never recover. But even as he had sobbed into his pillow, he had felt a particle of comfort knowing his sister was in the next room doing the same thing. This was different. This time he was absolutely alone. His two best friends, the only people on earth he really trusted, had betrayed him. He had no other close relationships. He talked to his father only once or twice a year, and hadn't heard from his sister since college.

For the first time in his life he briefly

contemplated suicide. Why not? Who would care? He toyed with the idea, weighing the advantages and disadvantages of different methods. Mechanically he got up and slowly headed for the bathroom. Death was so final. Should he take more time to consider other options? It was Friday, and he had Saturday off. If he could just get through the day, he could think it through over the weekend.

After picking up his mailbag at the post office, Nick took off on his route. The routine, seeing familiar people at each stop, combined with the physical activity of walking, seemed to dull the pain and help him forget his circumstances. But as he climbed onto his bike after work and headed home, the words Jessica had written came back to him. He pedaled faster, trying to escape his anger and despair.

Nick stopped at a deli, picked up a sandwich, and headed back outside. Near the bike rack stood a smiling young man, obviously waiting for someone.

"Hi! Here is something you really ought to read!" The young man held out a paper to Nick.

Nick scanned the words on the front of the

tract. "Christ Is the Answer!" The sheer naiveté annoyed him.

"Don't you think it's a little stupid to go telling random people what the answer is before determining their question? If I walked up to you and said the answer is five without listening to and understanding your question, wouldn't you think I'm out of my mind?"

Shaking his head, Nick mounted his bike. But the young man wasn't finished. Ignoring Nick's response, he cheerfully continued, "Sir, did you know God loves you and has a great plan for your life?"

Rage surged through Nick. He felt like grabbing the young man and shaking that smile off his face. After that, he'd rip all his nice little preconceived notions apart and show him how weak his arguments were. How could this teenager, probably just out of high school, presume to understand the complexity of his situation and then give him a pretty little piece of paper that supposedly provided a solution?

Kicking his bike into motion, Nick suppressed his urge to lash back. He replied tersely over his shoulder, "No thanks. I have my own plan for my life."

Wind in his face, Nick replayed the interaction. Religious people could be so ignorant. How could anyone be so blind? In light of all the evidence to the contrary, how could that young man still believe in a god? Especially one who loves people. Nick snorted. The world was full of problems and pain. If this wonderful god existed, why didn't he do something about it? Why should people carry little papers around to placate others with a feel-good lie about a god who loves them, and then everything is supposed to be okay? If he had his way, these people would be jailed for spreading propaganda!

Still fuming, Nick arrived at his apartment building. What was he supposed to do now? Sit alone and watch television? Find some stupid chatroom and communicate with lonely, self-absorbed people?

Jerking open the stairway door, Nick started up the stairs. He was just rounding the first landing when the rear bicycle wheel caught on the handrail, wrenching the bike from his grip and almost knocking him down. The bicycle clattered down the stairs and crashed on the wooden floor below.

Nick cussed and followed, stooping to survey the damage. Several spokes hung at rakish angles to each other. Part of the brake cable had torn.

Nick kicked the lowest stair. Here was his bike, not even paid off yet, and now damaged beyond his ability to fix it, all because of his carelessness. *What a fitting finale to a terrible week!* he thought. *Every time I think things can't get worse, they do! So much for my plans for a leisurely Saturday morning to contemplate my future. Instead, I'll have to pay a visit to Andy's Bike Shop.*

CHAPTER THREE

AS A POSTAL WORKER, Nick had an intimate view into the lives of people within his community. The magazines and catalogs they received, the frequency of their vacations, and even the quantity of their mail revealed much. Nick couldn't help but be curious about the personal life of Andy Mullins, the bike repairman, who lived in an apartment above his small shop. Andy received an unusual amount of mail. And the bulk of it was not flyers and advertisements; it was private correspondence from diverse locations. Nick didn't have any other stops quite like this one.

Early the next morning Nick walked his bike the three blocks to Andy's shop. Since he had no contact with Andy other than saying hello each day as he dropped off the mail, Nick really didn't know much about him, but the man seemed friendly and approachable.

When he entered the shop, Nick saw Andy talking with an older lady at the back of the store. Neither of them noticed his presence, so Nick leaned his bike against the wall and began looking at cycling accessories. He had been wanting a different bike seat. As he compared the options along the wall, Nick couldn't help overhearing the conversation in the back of the shop. The woman was sharing her personal problems. Her words, though quiet, carried easily in the empty shop. Ironically, they echoed his own thoughts.

"Sometimes I wonder why I should keep living. Why not take a bunch of pain pills and end it all?"

Curious, Nick inched toward their conversation.

"My family wouldn't miss me. Neither of my children even called at Christmas. Jim died over five years ago, and the last time I was in the hospital, you were the only one who visited me."

The shop was silent. Andy, restocking shelves, didn't respond.

"Maybe if I had money or were leaving an inheritance, people would care."

Nick realized he was eavesdropping and felt a twinge of guilt. He wasn't sure what to do. Should he shuffle his feet or cough to let them know he was there? Yet he wanted to hear the rest of the conversation. This woman was verbalizing his own loneliness and rejection. Nick trained his eyes on the display of colored water bottles, wondering how Andy would respond.

Instead, the woman continued. "I know what you are going to say. That God cares about me and loves me, and that I should learn to know and trust him. Somehow when I talk to you, God seems very real. But when I get back home, he seems so distant."

She paused before continuing. "I still have that Bible you gave me. Maybe I should try reading it. I don't know what else to do."

The woman's sad voice trailed off as she slowly turned and took a step toward the front door, but Andy stopped her. "Wait."

He walked to the workshop behind the store, returning with a small plate of cookies. Handing it to her, he said quietly, "Here's a little something for you. One of the church families dropped it off, and they have given us much more than we need. Just remember, you are loved, and you are not alone."

Her face brightened as she took the plate, yet she protested, "You are always giving me things. I can't keep doing this!"

Just then Andy noticed Nick. Quietly he spoke a few words to the woman. When she had gone, he called out to Nick, "Can I help you?" Nick showed Andy his bike. Carrying the bike to his workshop in the rear, Andy mounted it on a repair stand and examined the damage. "The brakes can be repaired, but we'll have to order new spokes." Andy searched on his computer for the replacement parts.

While he waited, Nick mulled over the discussion he had just overheard. Evidently Andy was a Christian—one of those ignorant people who believed in a god he couldn't see. The woman had asked some good questions, but Andy didn't seem to have any good answers.

"I couldn't help but hear your discussion with that woman. She has real problems. Yet instead of solutions, you gave her a few cookies. What's she supposed to do when the cookies are gone?"

Nick had meant to be polite, but he was unable to keep the sarcasm from his voice. He waited to see how Andy would respond, but when he merely acknowledged Nick's words with a brief smile and kept typing, Nick continued with a condescending smirk. "Actually, sharing cookies was better than telling her to trust in a nonexistent god. At least she can eat the cookies."

Again Nick paused, wondering why Andy didn't push back. Maybe Andy recognized the hollowness of his remarks.

Nick stepped out of the way as a woman came into the shop and set a plate of food on a table, exchanged a few words with Andy, and then left. Andy, still working on the computer, didn't seem inclined to respond to Nick's arguments, so Nick pressed further.

"Belief in a supreme being sounds wonderful to many simple-minded people. But when life gets difficult, a fictitious god won't solve real problems in real people's lives."

Nick left his challenge hanging in the air. Andy finished his work and then responded calmly without looking up, "Sounds reasonable. Why trust in something that doesn't exist?"

Nick wasn't sure how to respond, but before he could speak, Andy pointed to his computer. "I found a source for the spokes, but it will take a week or so to get them in. Your bike is a limited edition, so parts are hard to find."

For a moment Andy pursed his lips in thought. Then he turned on his stool and looked directly into Nick's eyes. With obvious concern he asked, "Are you facing some problems?"

The unexpected question took Nick off guard. He barely knew this man. Judging from the plaques hanging on the walls, he must be religious, but he didn't act like the other religious fanatics he'd met. *I should tell him to mind his own business,* Nick thought. *But, hey, why not just give him a taste of reality?*

So he did. Nick unloaded all the problems he was facing. He didn't leave anything out. Starting all the way back with Sunday school and his introduction to a fairytale god, Nick dumped his life story. He told of his mother running off with a man from church, bringing Nick to the conclusion that Christians were hypocrites and that belief in a god was just a convenient crutch for people who couldn't handle reality. He described the plans he and Jessica had made, how his best friend Eric had betrayed him, and how both had deserted him. Now he found himself alone, without family or friends.

As he talked, Nick paced around the little workshop, his voice rising with frustration. Pointing to a sign on the wall, he concluded, "Look at that crazy sign saying that God is good. Good for what? If there is a god, why doesn't he do something? Your imaginary god might be weak or he might be wicked. But don't try telling me he is good! If he exists, he sure isn't doing anything about my problems!"

Nick was shouting at Andy now, and he wasn't finished.

"My landlord called yesterday wondering why the rent wasn't paid. He doesn't care whether my girlfriend—ex-girlfriend—stole the money or not. He just wants his money. And do you know who he is? He's another hypocritical Christian. He has a sign on his Mercedes-Benz saying, 'Christians aren't perfect, just forgiven!' Now I come in here, and you tell me my bike won't be ready for a week. How am I supposed to get to work? And where is this wonderful, good god you want me to believe in when I need him?"

Embarrassed and angry because he had lost control, Nick scribbled his contact information on a piece of paper, slammed it on the desk, and gave one parting shot. "Call me when my bike's fixed. But don't try telling me about a good god. And don't give me cookies!"

CHAPTER FOUR

NICK LAUGHED as he strode home. *I sure set Andy straight! With a nice little business and most likely a wife and family who care for him, it was high time Mr. Preacher-man listened to some real problems.*

But he didn't laugh long. His problems weren't over. He still needed transportation to get to work Monday morning, and then there was the rent. The landlord said he needed the money within a few days, and Nick's paycheck wouldn't come till the end of next week.

His jaw set, he climbed the steps to his apartment. As he reached the door, his phone beeped. Pulling it out, he read the text message:

> *I won't be using my bike next week, if that would help.* —*Andy*

It was a small thing, yet the unexpected kindness hit Nick like a punch in the stomach, knocking the anger out of him. He felt as though he had been stumbling through a pitch-black room filled with obstacles, when suddenly a pinpoint of light provided a tiny spark of hope. Andy might be a religious freak, but at least he was a nice one.

Lying in his lonely bed that night, Nick stared at the ceiling as he thought back over his interaction with the shopkeeper. There were two scenes Nick couldn't erase from his mind.

The first was Andy's response to him. Andy had simply asked if Nick was having any difficulties. He had responded by insulting Andy's intelligence, ridiculing his religious beliefs, and mocking his kindness in giving a plate of cookies to an old lady. Nick shifted uncomfortably. If someone had treated him that way, he would have been out for blood. But Andy hadn't argued or responded unkindly. Nick had even seen a tear running down Andy's face at the end of his tirade. He wished he had spoken a little more calmly.

But the second scene produced a stronger reaction in Nick. In fact, just thinking about it now made him furious. It was the sign hanging over

Andy's desk. It proclaimed:

GOD IS GOOD

Nick wasn't sure why that sign made him so angry. As he lay in bed, he tried to analyze his feelings. Was it because the sign, confidently flying in the face of scientific evidence, asserted that there was a god? Was it the ridiculous assumption that this supposed all-powerful god is good? Or was he annoyed simply because this man, with his easy life, was ignoring all the pain and suffering in the world, covering it over with a sign proclaiming that all is well?

Sleep came slowly as Nick tossed and turned, and it was close to noon before he awoke the next day. He sat around trying to interest himself in various sitcoms, but his mind kept going to Jessica. *I wonder what she is doing. Would there be any possible way to redeem myself? Is she with Eric right now?* He reached for another beer.

Monday morning arrived, and Nick found himself mechanically marching through another day. With nothing to look forward to other than carrying mail, coming home to a lonely house, and pleading with the landlord for mercy, his normal ambition had evaporated. That evening he wearily climbed the stairs with Andy's bike, secretly hoping the landlord had forgotten about the rent.

No such luck. Before he reached his apartment, he could see the notice taped to the door. Yanking it off as he passed through, Nick leaned the bike against the wall and crashed into his chair. He sat for a moment, procrastinating, dreading the contents. He knew what it would say—if you can't come up with the money, then move out. His grace period was past, and nothing but money he didn't have would suffice.

Tearing open the envelope, he read the note. His jaw dropped.

> *Nick,*
> *A man stopped in today and paid last month's rent. He wanted to remain anonymous, but your account is paid to date. He said he just wanted to help you out.*
> *We would encourage you to not let this happen again.*
> *—All Star Property Management*

Nick rubbed his forehead. Was this a joke? Whoever heard of an anonymous donor paying someone else's rent? The only person aware of his rent situation was Jessica. His heart gave a sudden leap. Might she have had a change of heart? But no, the note said it was a man. Suddenly Nick remembered Andy. Could he have done it?

Heading back down the stairs, Nick rode down to the bike shop. He found Andy singing while he worked in the back. Forgoing pleasantries, Nick went straight to the point.

"Andy, do you know anything about someone paying my rent?"

"Paying your rent? No. I remember you saying you were in trouble, and if it wasn't paid immediately, you would need to move out. Someone else paid it?"

"Yes! When I arrived home this evening, a note was on the door, but instead of an eviction notice, it said an anonymous person had paid my rent!"

Both stared at each other, foreheads creased. Then suddenly a look of understanding flitted across Andy's face.

"Ah! I think I know what might have happened."

"You do?"

"Maybe. Several men from our church on Fifth Street meet Sunday mornings before church for prayer. We pray, sharing needs and concerns. Maybe I shouldn't have, but I mentioned your situation and some of the problems you are facing. I didn't say your name, but afterward one of the men asked me privately if anything could be done to help. I told him about your rent situation, and he asked for your name and apartment complex. That's all I know."

"You think he paid it?"

"It's possible. It isn't uncommon for this kind of thing to happen."

A customer came in the front door, and Andy went to help. Nick remained leaning against the counter in stunned silence. This was wild! Paying rent for someone you didn't even know? He'd never heard of anything like that. What was the proper response when someone anonymously paid your rent? Just go on? Act like it's normal? But what really puzzled him was Andy's response. He hadn't even acted shocked. He just casually said something about this kind of thing not being uncommon. *Yeah, right!*

Glancing above Andy's desk, he stared again

at that sign. Andy would probably say that some good god was involved. A wry smile crossed Nick's face. He knew better. There might be a few unusually good people out there. But an all-powerful, good god? If that were true, a whole lot of things would be different in the world.

As he waited for Andy to return, Nick suddenly realized that the conversation in the back of the store had nothing to do with bikes. A boy was talking to Andy earnestly. He was obviously having difficulty at home. He spoke of his father leaving home. Nick could hear the pain in his voice.

Nick found himself drawn into the conversation. He identified with the boy's agony. The boy was sobbing as he spoke. Nick knew exactly how he felt. Listening to Andy's kind response, his heart twisted. What would it have been like if he'd had someone like Andy to talk to after his mother left?

Heading back home, Nick had much to ponder. That boy's story had awakened emotions and memories. Andy's thoughtful and caring comments had piqued his curiosity. *I'm not sure what to do with all this*, he thought, *but one thing is certain. This Andy is different from any other religious freak I've ever met!*

CHAPTER FIVE

THERE WAS A CHILL in the morning air as Nick delivered mail the next day. Leaves were beginning to fall, and the days were brisk and pleasant. So much had happened in the past few days, and he appreciated the chance to think. Nick wondered if Andy had received a delivery date on his bike spokes, but there were too many customers in the store when he delivered Andy's mail to ask about it then. He couldn't help but wonder just who had paid his rent. Andy had said he went to a church on Fifth Street, but that wasn't much of a clue. Nick delivered mail in that area and couldn't remember ever seeing a church there.

That evening he stopped in at Andy's bike shop after work. Hearing a discussion in the back, Nick walked toward the shop area. A mother and her young son were just leaving.

"I don't know how to thank you. This means so much to us right now!" Her voice choked as the excited boy pushed his new bike toward the door.

"Take good care of it, and it'll last you quite a while," Andy told the boy with a smile. "And if you decide you want the seat lower, stop in. It isn't hard to adjust."

The two left the store, but the woman's emotional comment stirred Nick's curiosity. People didn't normally purchase a product and then tearfully thank the seller.

"Do all your customers thank you for allowing them to purchase bikes from your shop?"

Andy, seated at his desk, glanced up with a smile. "She was extremely nice, wasn't she?" Then, in an abrupt change of subject, "I just received an email saying your spokes should be in by the end of the week. Is my bike working out okay in the meantime?"

"It's working great." Nick was still curious about this woman, and he was pretty sure he wasn't getting the entire story. But he also had a distinct feeling he wasn't going to get more information from Andy.

"Thanks for the update on the spokes." Nick

turned to leave, but that crazy sign jumped out at him. Every time he came, that sign bothered him, and when he tried to sleep, it swam before his eyes. Something inside him wanted to expose the absurdity of the message. But he held back for two reasons. First, he was still a little embarrassed about how he had acted the first time he had talked to Andy about it. He was also confused by how unshaken Andy had been by the force of his compelling arguments. Nick would need to change his attitude before launching another attack. After all, the shopkeeper had been very decent.

"Andy, that first time I came in, I shouted at you and wasn't respectful. I'm sorry. I guess I was under so much stress that everything came out wrong."

Andy looked up from his desk with a smile. "Don't feel bad, Nick. I'm just glad you felt comfortable sharing your struggles. All of us have difficulties, and I have said many things I've regretted later. I don't think you really meant everything you said anyway, at least not once you had time to think things through logically."

Andy turned back to his desk, and Nick was

afraid he had been misunderstood.

"Let me be clear. I'm not saying I don't believe what I said about the existence of a god. But I should have explained myself without shouting. I still don't believe a good god exists. But I think that's obvious to most thinking people."

Andy calmly walked across the shop to get a paper before returning to his desk. "No problem, Nick, and no hard feelings. But now that you've calmed down, why don't you explain why you don't believe a good god exists?"

Nick stood watching Andy work. Was this man really prepared for an intellectual debate? Hadn't he ever been exposed to truth? Had he been brainwashed as a child and never taught about evolution, science, and the weight of evidence against a real god? Maybe he was not aware that the only people out there who still believed in religious myths were morons who refused to face facts.

"Sure, Andy, I don't mind explaining why I don't believe in a god. For one thing, I'm only interested in truth. I'm not creating an imaginary being to fill some inner need. I would love to discover that there is a god out there who loves me. Who wouldn't? Every culture has dreamed up imaginary deities to fill that internal urge. But just the fact that all the religions contradict each other shows that religion comes from people rather than observation of facts. Surely you can see that, Andy."

The shopkeeper, still working at his desk, responded after a short pause. "So your first point is that differences in religion demonstrate that God is a product of man's imagination. What else?"

"Second, even if there were an all-powerful god as Christians insist, he couldn't be good. Look at the suffering in the world. Think about it, Andy. If you could instantly stop all the pain in this world, wouldn't you do it? Of course you would! You get together on Sunday mornings to pray to God, and what do you ask? You ask him to intervene in people's lives, don't you? Someone is sick, someone else has lost a job, and some husband has run off with another woman. All these things create pain, and you would like to see that suffering stop. Isn't that correct?"

Andy was obviously listening, but since he didn't respond, Nick continued. "And yet you also say that this god already knows everything and is in total control. He could heal the sick, resolve all the employment issues, and reconcile all the messed-up relationships. And yet he doesn't do it! You want me to believe in a god like that? Even if a god exists, he obviously doesn't love people as much as your little group does. At least you would like to relieve the suffering."

Again Nick paused, waiting for a response before pressing on. "Maybe you haven't thought about all this. I understand. Remember, I was raised in a Christian home, and it wasn't till I got away from my mother's brainwashing that I was able to see truth. I am sure your parents brain-washed you as well, and maybe you haven't ex-perienced the pain that others have. I can accept that. We haven't all had the same experiences. It's possible to grow up in a nice, cozy environment and come to all kinds of conclusions about some Jesus who loves you. But you aren't a child any-more. It's time you look at some of life's cold, hard facts, Andy." Then, pointing at the sign, he added, "Especially before hanging up trite state-ments about God being good."

Andy didn't say anything for a moment. With a glance at his watch, he started putting papers away. "Thanks for sharing, Nick. I appreciate your openness and would like to hear more. But I told my wife I would be upstairs as soon as possible. I have an idea—how about meeting tomorrow evening for pizza? I can tell there's more on your mind, and perhaps you'd also like to hear a little of my story." Then with a smile the shop owner concluded, "I might even explain why that sign is there."

CHAPTER SIX

NICK GRABBED a frozen dinner, threw it in the oven, and took a shower. *I wonder what Andy is having for dinner,* he thought as he forked in a mouthful of his tasteless pasta dish. As he had left the bike shop, a lady had come in carrying a dish of something that smelled delicious. Nick stopped chewing, staring off into space. Several times he had seen people bring food to Andy's shop. What was with all the food?

Nick smiled. Just one more mystery in the life of this strange shopkeeper.

The following night Nick was a little nervous as he arrived at Mario's Pizza Shop. His only interaction with Andy had been at the bike shop, so meeting in this setting seemed strange. He grinned wryly. Joining religious do-gooders for dinner wasn't his general practice. But he was curious about Andy's past. Why did he choose to believe in something that society—at least the thinking segment of it—had dismissed? Maybe he just had nice religious parents he didn't want to disappoint.

Andy arrived a few minutes late, and they selected a corner booth. Nick assumed Andy would be ready to argue some point from the previous night, but he didn't seem in a hurry. Instead he asked about Nick's day. He asked how he was feeling about Jessica's departure and how work was going. Nick wasn't sure how it happened, but Andy's disarming questions caused him to open up and share about his loneliness and anger. He was a little shocked at how comfortable he was talking to Andy, and when the pizza arrived, Nick suddenly realized that Andy still hadn't revealed anything about his own life.

Nick reached for his second piece of pizza. "So, Andy, you keep asking about my life, but what about yours? You still believe in a god out there, even though the rest of the world has progressed beyond such myths. Why do you insist on ignoring scientific proof? Did you have persuasive parents or an unusually good Sunday school teacher?"

Andy laughed as he wiped his mouth. "No. You see, Nick, I never went to Sunday school. I never even attended a church till I was about your age."

"Come on, Andy, not even for Easter or Christmas?"

"No, but maybe I should start at the beginning. I grew up in a home where religion was scoffed at and viewed as a crutch for those incapable of rational thought. In fact, if I had closed my eyes the other night when you expressed your skepticism, I could have been back home listening to my father. He hated religion, especially Christianity. So as far back as I can remember, I was taught Darwinism, naturalism, and humanism. My father wanted me to grow up without ever coming under the influence of religious teaching, and for the most part he succeeded."

"But that's impossible! How could anyone come to believe in God without someone pounding that ideology into him?"

Andy wiped his hands. "Let me go on. All those who impacted my life—my teachers, my friends, and of course my parents—were opposed to religion. They all laughed at the concept of God. I was taught to love science. Further, I was taught that all answers can be found in science, which relies on what is tangible, rather than in crazy religions, which focus on the unseen. And yet, ironically, it was in science class that I experienced my first doubts. My eighth-grade teacher was talking about the expanding universe. He was explaining once again how everything started with the big bang. In my mind I pictured this incomprehensible explosion, and then, probably because I had been raised to question everything, I began to ponder the cause. In other words, we kept focusing on what happened *after* that huge explosion, but I wanted to know what brought the forces together to create it?"

Andy chuckled before continuing. "The more I thought about it, this big bang just happening without cause seemed ludicrous. I wondered what would happen if suddenly there were a huge explosion outside. The classroom windows would shake, things would fly by, and the air would be filled with smoke. I tried to imagine how my teacher would respond if I told him there had been no cause for that explosion. It just happened. He wouldn't have believed me, and if I had maintained my position, he would have flunked me for poor logic. Explosions don't just happen without something causing them. Everyone knows that, yet here we were in class being told that this gigantic explosion happened billions of years ago, but there was nothing behind it. There was no cause; it just happened!"

"But Andy, the universe is expanding, and the only conceivable explanation is that there was a big bang."

"Remember, Nick, I am just sharing my story. Let me go on. The next thing I had to deal with was the precision and order that came out of this explosion."

Andy threw back his head and laughed. "Have you ever watched something explode? I mean a huge explosion? Have you ever seen anything orderly or precise come out of that? Even once?"

Nick shook his head. "No, but science doesn't say the universe was immediately arranged as we know it."

"You're right. We are told that it took billions of years for things to gradually develop and improve. But to my young mind, this made the theory even more absurd. Do you see things improving over time in our natural world? Every single thing we produce or develop immediately begins to deteriorate unless someone diligently maintains it."

"You mean the second law of thermodynamics?" Nick replied thoughtfully.

"Exactly. And here's what confused me. On the one hand I was taught that things evolved and kept getting better over time—that this evolutionary process is so powerful that it can take the mess of an explosion and make a beautiful, intricate universe. All you need to do is give it enough time." Andy spread his hands. "But on the other hand we were being told the opposite. We were also supposed to believe that everything deteriorates over time. So as more time elapses and the earth is subjected to this law of entropy, the worse things become. Can you see why I was confused? And even worse, my teachers were telling me to believe only what could be observed and proven. I could observe the law of entropy. It was all around me. I could also see microevolution—like viruses that adapt to resist antibiotics. But I couldn't see examples of macroevolution. I couldn't find any reliable cases of creatures changing from one species, or kind, to another."

The pizza had been forgotten, and when the

waitress brought the bill, they suddenly became aware of the passing of time.

"Before we go, Nick, let me share one more issue I dealt with as a young man. Imagine living in a house with many rooms. As a child, you freely roam the house and are allowed to play in any room. But there is one exception—your parents forbid you to enter one room at the end of the hall. You can go into any other room and do whatever you wish. But you are not supposed to ever open that one door at the end of the hall. What would you eventually be tempted to do?"

"I would be extremely curious what was behind that door!"

"Exactly! For me, religion was that door. My parents were thrilled to see me explore evolutionary science, naturalism, humanism, philosophy—you name it. It didn't matter how absurd the theory, they viewed the study of all those as part of getting a well-rounded education. But they were adamant that I stay away from religion of any kind."

"So you turned to religion out of curiosity?"

Andy chuckled. "That might have had something to do with why I finally opened the door and peeked into that room. But ironically, it was my parents' teaching that caused me to walk in and investigate further. From the beginning they had encouraged me to think for myself and ask hard questions. 'Keep digging,' they told me, 'until you find truth.' Obviously they weren't happy with where that search eventually took me. But I wasn't finding satisfactory answers to my questions about origins of the universe. As I listened to my teachers and parents, I noticed some major gaps in their logic. Millions or even billions of years do not answer many hard questions regarding origins. Neither does the fact that everyone was parroting the illogical conclusions they'd been taught. My parents had told me to never assume that truth was with the majority. So not finding solid answers eventually forced me to look elsewhere. Eventually I had to peek behind that door."

Nick sat in stunned silence. This was not what he had expected. He had been sure Andy was brainwashed as a child. He would have bet any amount of money on it. There was so much more he wanted to ask. But he wasn't quite happy with where the discussion was leading.

"I can understand your curiosity, Andy. But just because you found holes in evolution doesn't prove there is a god. Maybe science will eventually discover what caused the big bang."

"You're right. Just because you can poke holes in someone else's theory doesn't mean your own is logical or correct." He glanced at his watch. "I have to go, but let's get together and talk more."

Getting up from the table, Andy put money down for the tip and looked at Nick with a mischievous grin. "And who knows, we might eventually even get around to why that sign you dislike is hanging on my shop wall!"

CHAPTER SEVEN

NICK FELT A BIT disconcerted as he pondered the discussion with Andy the night before. Was it possible that God might be the cause behind the universe? He zipped his coat against the fall breeze and tried to shrug off the annoying thought. But could the detailed, orderly way nature worked be explained logically by a huge explosion, natural selection, and survival of the fittest? And then there was the way Andy had arrived at his conclusions. He'd come to believe in God as Creator by carefully observing facts and challenging the status quo.

Looking around at the dependable changes the fall season brought, Nick could see how a person might conclude there was a designer. He recalled youthful doubts about how incredibly complex things such as the human eye could have just evolved. But something inside him still rebelled against believing that this designer was inherently good. He had seen far too much pain and human suffering in life to ever accept that.

Alone in his thoughts, he suddenly noticed a bike coming toward him. As he stepped off the sidewalk to let it pass, he recognized the boy who had purchased the bike from Andy.

"Hey, how do you like your new bike?"

The boy stopped and turned around before responding with a grin. "It's great! Hey, I saw you at the bike shop."

Curious about the rest of the story, Nick asked, "Had you been wanting a bike for a while?"

"Yeah, but my mom doesn't have much money. It's kind of a long story." The boy looked down, scuffing his sneaker against the sidewalk.

"My dad left home a while back. He ran off with some other woman, and my mom has to go out and clean houses and stuff to pay the bills. Mom wanted me to have a bike so I could deliver newspapers and help earn some money. She said all of us were going to need to work to make ends meet. I was willing to work, but we couldn't afford a bike. Somehow Mr. Andy heard about it, I guess, and he gave me this one. He goes to that church over on Fifth Street. Do you ever go there?"

Nick shook his head, and the boy rambled on. "We don't either, but they are really nice. Mom says she doesn't know how we would have survived without them. They bring us food and other stuff we need. They even brought us some clothes. Well, I need to get going. My mom's waiting. See ya!"

Hands on his hips, Nick watched the boy continue down the sidewalk. He knew by now that Andy was unusually generous. And he knew there was another generous man out there who had paid his rent. But a whole group of Andys? Who were these people? Nick shook his head and continued on his mail route.

Saturday evening found Nick in Andy's workshop. Andy wanted to stay close to home in case his wife needed anything, so he had picked up Chinese food and invited Nick over. Nick had never met Andy's wife. In fact, he still knew very little about Andy's personal life other than what he had shared over pizza. As the two men sat down around a workbench to eat, Nick determined to uncover more of the mystery behind this shopkeeper.

"The other night you explained briefly why you decided to open that door of religion and take a peek. As you know, I'm not convinced there's evidence for the existence of a god. But I am intrigued by your story. There are two specific questions I have been rolling around. First, how did you decide that God, if there is one, is good? In other words, if one does exist, how can he be good while allowing pain and suffering? And second, of all the religions out there, why Christianity? How do you know that the Christianity of the Bible is true?"

"Fair enough, Nick, but let me start with your second question—why Christianity, and how do I know that the Bible is true?"

Andy set his food down and leaned back against the wall. "If you have never tried opening the door of religion, that first peek can be daunting! It's hard to know where to start, so I tried to give every religion due diligence. But there's one thing I need to be clear about before we go further, Nick: I still can't prove the existence of God."

Nick looked surprised. "But I thought that was what you were going to do."

"No. I can only share my experience, the evidence I have considered, and why I have chosen to believe in Jesus Christ. Let me ask you, can you prove that George Washington actually lived? Can you prove that the stories we read, the famous portraits, or even his home at Mount Vernon aren't all forgeries?"

"Well, no, I can't prove it, but the evidence is overwhelming. There's no question that he lived!"

"I agree, and yet you can't prove it. You have taken the facts that are available, considered them, and chosen to believe. That's exactly where I am with Jesus Christ. I can't prove that he lived, died, or rose to life again. I can't even prove that he ever existed. But I have reviewed the available facts, observed his impact on my life and on the lives of others, and I believe without reservation that he is who he said he is. But remember, I can't prove it."

"But how did you arrive at that conclusion? And why Christianity above all other religions?"

"I began with one premise. For the most part, we live in a world of logic and predictability. If you plant corn, you don't get tomatoes. So I started my search believing that the great designer, whoever that is, must have had a purpose. There is something behind all this complexity. You follow me?"

"I'm listening." Nick tried to keep his body language casual to hide his growing discomfort.

"You keep mentioning human suffering, and I struggled with that as well. Men have always wrestled with suffering, and every religion has its own spin on it. Naturalism, which I was taught as a child, says everything is an accident. Suffering is bad luck, but has no meaning. Eastern religions insinuate that suffering is just an illusion, so the best we can do is find ways to ignore it. Bad things happen to us because of bad karma accumulated from past lives, so we are ultimately responsible for the pain we experience. Not much comfort there. Buddhism teaches that the highest state a man can reach is nirvana, or a place where neither suffering nor joy exists. No bad, but no good either. That seemed ridiculous. Imagine a god of purpose designing a universe so bad that the best a person can do is escape from it!"

Nick shrugged, looking down at the shop floor. "I don't know. Maybe Buddha was on to something. Arriving at a place of nothingness can sound pretty good at times. But keep going."

"Islam teaches that everything, including pain and suffering, is caused by Allah. He is the ultimate source of everything we know. He is all-wise, and our job is simply to submit to his will. Not much of an explanation."

Andy paused to gather his thoughts. "In short, I found all these religions' attempts to explain why suffering exists woefully inadequate. In every one of them, God seemed distant and uninvolved. There didn't seem to be any logical explanation or redemptive purpose for pain and suffering."

Andy took a drink of soda before continuing. "In Christianity I found something completely different. The God of the Bible doesn't ignore our suffering. Quite the opposite. He not only acknowledges pain and suffering, but enters into it himself. That was a shocker! We find God's son, Jesus, coming as a man and weeping with those who are in pain, showing compassion to society's outcasts, and even allowing himself to be beaten, rejected, and crucified. Clearly he wanted to experience what his creation was experiencing on an earth corrupted by man's sin. This seemed beyond what any man could dream up—that God, who is big enough to do whatever he wanted, would care about human suffering so deeply that he would enter into it himself on man's level. Amazing!" Andy's eyes sparked with enthusiasm.

Nick had never heard Christianity explained quite like this. More questions came to his mind, but he wasn't sure where to start. Linking his hands on the tabletop, Nick looked up at Andy. "Your way of explaining your faith puts it in a new light. But I still have some major questions."

Andy nodded. "I understand, Nick. Even after all these years, I still have questions. But the Bible assures us of this: eventually everything will be made right. Evil will be punished, good will be rewarded, and we will discover that there was purpose in what we suffered. We will know that God actually intended good to come out of pain and suffering."

Nick stared at Andy. "I wonder if you could say all that if you were going through everything I am. I don't think you could hold that view if you were experiencing real pain and suffering!"

"Maybe not, Nick, but I wish you would come back tomorrow night. I really want you to meet my wife." Andy glanced at the wall. "And that sign—I almost forgot. Maybe we can finally get around to explaining why it's hanging there."

CHAPTER EIGHT

NICK DROPPED OFF THE MAIL at Andy's shop and was heading out the door when Andy called after him, "Don't forget to come over tonight. Be here around six and eat with us."

Nick responded with a nod and a wave. He was actually looking forward to it. He enjoyed his talks with Andy and the thoughts they sparked. But Andy had said little about his family. Was his wife religious too? Did they have children? Andy must be over forty years old.

Nick was also curious about this church on Fifth Street. He'd looked carefully, even checking the mail registry, but couldn't find anything. Hopefully tonight he would get some answers.

Nick arrived that evening to find the shopkeeper finishing up some last-minute tasks. Opening a door in the back, Andy waved him up the stairway. To Nick's surprise, music met his ears. Entering the small upstairs apartment, he saw a group of eight to ten young people standing around a hospital bed, singing with joyful enthusiasm. As the song ended, the singers said goodbye to the woman in the bed, nodded hello to Andy and Nick, and disappeared down the stairs.

Nick watched them go and then turned his attention to the invalid. Her face was gaunt and almost gray, yet her eyes sparkled. Andy walked to the bed. "Teresa, this is my friend Nick. Nick, meet my wife and best friend, Teresa."

"Hello, Teresa, it's nice to meet you," Nick stammered. "I didn't realize that Andy had a sick wife. I shouldn't have been taking his evenings away from you."

Teresa laughed softly. "Andy wouldn't have missed his times with you for anything. He always comes back from meeting people and gives me a full report. That helps me know how to pray for people in the community. And Nick, I have been praying for you. I have dealt with physical suffering for many years. But I know from experience that the inner suffering you are going through can be even more intense."

Nick wasn't sure how to respond. He felt awkward around sick people, and this woman was obviously very ill.

Andy headed for the kitchen. "I'll heat some food while you get acquainted."

Teresa, noticing Nick's discomfort, moved on with the conversation. "Andy said he hadn't told you about my situation, so you were probably shocked to see a woman in a hospital bed."

Nick smiled a little. "You're right. I wasn't expecting that."

Teresa continued, "While he gets some food, let me share my story. Andy and I met in college. We came from similar backgrounds. His parents were big into education, and mine into business and wealth. We married with hopes and dreams of having a family. We wanted children who felt loved and cared for, and maybe even a nice place out in the country where the children could roam and enjoy the outdoors."

Teresa shifted in bed, a stab of pain briefly crossing her face. "I think Andy already shared our spiritual journey. Mine was very similar to his, and it was shortly after we both committed to following Jesus that I was diagnosed with cancer. That was a huge blow. Our families had both written us off by this time, and we felt very alone and abandoned. After receiving treatment for my cancer, I was told I wouldn't be able to have children."

Andy came in carrying a tray of food. He smiled at Teresa. "I see you didn't waste any time. Can you pause your story long enough to eat?"

Andy pulled two chairs over to the bed, and he and Teresa bowed their heads while Andy said a brief prayer of thanksgiving. He had done this the other times he and Nick had eaten together, and though Nick wasn't accustomed to the practice, he observed that praying seemed natural for Andy.

The prayer finished, Nick said, "Sorry for making you prepare food, Andy. I didn't even know you could cook."

"I can't! But you don't need to feel bad. Our freezer has so much food, we need help eating it."

Suddenly the truth dawned on Nick. "Is this some of the food people have been bringing into your shop? I've been trying to figure out what is going on. Who are these people?"

Andy passed a plate to Nick. "It's just people from our church on Fifth Street. They keep us well supplied. Actually, they bring more than we can use, and sometimes we have to share it with others."

"Okay, where is this church on Fifth Street? I walk that street every day and haven't seen a church anywhere."

Andy grinned. "Yes, you would have difficulty locating it. We meet in the community building there on the corner of Elm. We used to meet in a basement, but as the crowd grew, we had to rent a larger facility."

"And the young people who were here singing are part of your group?"

"Yes. They have been such a blessing. Teresa's pain can be quite intense, and their visits provide something for her to look forward to. But Teresa, you haven't finished telling our story."

Teresa, who didn't seem to be hungry, looked at Andy and smiled. "Okay, I'll try to make it brief. I survived that first round of cancer, but it has come back several times. Each time I've become weaker, and this time it is in my bones."

Her eyes rested lovingly on her husband as she concluded cheerfully, "But it looks like this will be the final round."

Nick felt disconcerted. She didn't look well at

all. Her eyes were sunken, and her voice was weak. How could she be so confident she would recover?

"So, the doctors are saying you'll have a full recovery?"

"No, Nick, the doctors aren't saying that at all. Last week they informed me there is nothing else they can do, and I probably have only a short time to live. Hospice has been taking good care of me, and Andy has been wonderful. Unless God steps in, I won't be alive much longer. But I have complete confidence in my God!"

Nothing in Nick's set of beliefs had prepared him for this. Here was a woman terminally ill, yet cheerful at the prospect of dying! Were these people really human? A glance over at Andy answered this question. Tears were running down his cheeks. Yes, they were human, but they clearly possessed something rare.

Teresa, noticing Nick's confusion, continued. "Nick, Andy has told me of your inner wrestling regarding God and specifically your questions about pain and suffering. I understand, and I can't say all my questions have been answered. But allow me to share a few of my thoughts."

Still wiping tears, Andy reached over and took

her hand.

"I have learned so much about God and myself through suffering," Teresa said. "It has been amazing! So much good has come from it. I have watched people lovingly bring hundreds of meals, cheerfully clean my home because I couldn't, and demonstrate the compassion of Jesus in more ways than I can explain. And that's not all. Almost every day we receive cards and letters from people I hardly know."

Nick listened in amazement. So that explained all the mail to this little bike shop! Teresa noticed his smile.

"Sorry for the added weight in your mailbag. You probably wondered why we were getting all that mail. And many of those envelopes had anonymous money orders or gift cards from someone wanting to share the love of God but not wanting to be personally recognized."

A tear trickled down her cheek as she looked over at Andy before continuing. "I am not trying to minimize the suffering. It has been long and intense. For me, it's almost over. But Andy may have years ahead of him. He will have hours of loneliness. But understand this—the same God who has been with me will be with him. The congregation that has supported me will continue supporting him. God is so good! I don't understand why I have cancer and why he allows some things to happen. I don't know why we were never able to have the children we longed for. But we have both seen his goodness in so many marvelous ways in the past that we are willing to trust him with our future and all the things we don't understand. God is good! Isn't that right, Andy?"

Looking into her face, Andy whispered, "That's right, dear."

Teresa wiped a tear from her husband's cheek. Then, looking at Nick with a bit of a mischievous smile, she concluded, "And just so there are no misunderstandings—Andy didn't hang that sign in the shop. I did!"

CHAPTER NINE

TERESA DIED just one week later. Nick, who a few weeks earlier couldn't have imagined sitting through a Christian funeral, found himself drawn there. Neighbors said it was to be held in a school gym. Nick wondered why. From what Andy had told him, their church group wasn't very large. Nick guessed fifty or sixty people might attend the funeral. But he was shocked when he found the gymnasium almost completely filled.

The lady sitting beside him had experienced a financial loss several years before. With tears she told him how Teresa had spent time praying with her and offering encouragement. Nick shuffled his feet uncomfortably but tried to listen respectfully. The man on the other side had a wayward son, and Andy had reached out to him. Nick looked around at the crowd. Did they all have stories like these? How could this one couple have impacted so many people?

After a short service, most of the people walked over to the public cemetery a few blocks away. As they walked, Nick asked people how they knew Andy and Teresa. It seemed everyone had a story. Some told of ways Andy had helped them, and others told how they had been inspired by Teresa's patience through years of suffering.

At all other graveside events Nick had attended, somebody had said a few words while several bored men sat on a backhoe in the distance, waiting for the mournful crowd to leave so they could finish their job. This was different. The church people sang hymns while filling the grave with shovels! He hunched his shoulders against the cold and studied their faces. He had never seen people fearlessly singing in the face of death. What was their secret?

As he rode his newly repaired bicycle home, Nick reflected on what he had just experienced. In some ways these people were just like everyone else. They shared tears and hugs. They were obviously going to miss Teresa, and they felt loss. Yet something was totally different. Even though they felt grief and disappointment, they had hope!

Nick had much to contemplate the next few days. He had listened to explanations that challenged his entire belief system, and he had watched someone approach death with peace and joy. He didn't know what to do with it all.

It wasn't long till he found himself drawn back to Andy's shop. After inquiring how Andy was dealing with his loss, Nick hesitantly moved on to his questions.

"Andy, I've been thinking about our discussions, and you've given me some profound things to consider. But questions keep rolling around in my mind. Why are you so different? Most Christians start by telling me I'm going to hell, asking me to accept Jesus into my life, and saying if I will just pray some little prayer, everything will be good between me and Jesus."

Andy sat for a moment with bowed head before answering. "Nick, I can't speak for others, but have you considered that God might be just as interested in getting heaven to earth as he is in getting men to heaven?"

Nick frowned. "What's that supposed to mean?"

"When Jesus lived here on earth, he didn't spend much time telling men how to get to heaven. That didn't seem to be his primary message. Make no mistake—there is a heaven and a hell. Yet it is possible to become so preoccupied with arguing over the best formula to save men from hell that we miss Jesus' primary message."

"Which was what?"

"Go back for a moment to your Sunday school lessons. Remember how God first created a perfect world? Then what happened?"

"Adam disobeyed God and ate some kind of fruit."

"That's right. Man rebelled against God, and the relationship between them was severed. Jesus came to earth to restore that lost relationship. Yet he didn't come only to tell men how to get right with God individually. His teachings circled around something he called the kingdom of God. He wanted a society of believers interacting, loving, and caring for each other and showing a broken world something radically different and beautiful. After your experience with Christians, this may be hard to believe. But go home and read your New Testament. Notice how many times Jesus talked about the kingdom of God."

Andy paused a moment before continuing.

"Sadly, this message has been lost by many. But Jesus came to reveal God's original intent for the world. He lived and taught the society of love God has always wanted his children to enjoy—a world where people love each other, aren't enamored by money or possessions, are merciful, and treat others like they want to be treated."

"But I thought the main Christian message was about Jesus dying and taking away our sins."

"That is essential to the message. Jesus died and rose triumphant over death so that we can have forgiveness of sins and a close relationship with God. But that is just the beginning! He also wants to empower every human to live as he lived. Jesus came to enable us to participate in this great kingdom he promoted."

"So how does church fit into all this?"

"Picture the globe, our world, in total darkness." Andy shaped a ball with his hands. "Imagine men living in this darkness. They are discouraged, tired, and unable to rise out of their desperate situation. They go through each day just trying to survive in a hopeless environment. All of this is a result of their disobedience, but they don't know that. So they continue groping about in the dark, drawing all kinds of wrong conclusions about God."

"You mean like imagining that an all-powerful god can't be good?" Nick asked wryly.

Andy laughed. "Exactly! So far away from truth, they can't picture a kind and benevolent Creator. Now imagine that the Creator wants to change this. What would he do?"

"I don't know. Maybe explain his original intent or send someone to show them something different?"

"Exactly! God tried repeatedly to explain himself. He sent prophets, demonstrated his power through the nation of Israel, and finally sent his Son to give an accurate picture of what God is really like. Through Christ's death and resurrection, he opened up a road back to the Father.

"When Jesus went back to his Father, he wanted his followers to continue this work of reconciling people to the Father. He envisioned little groups of redeemed and restored people, like torches around this dark globe, dispensing light from the Father. Churches are to be small communities of people committed to their Lord and each other, intently following the example of Jesus and demonstrating him collectively to a dark world.

When others watch how these people live, how they react, and how they love each other, it gets their attention. In the middle of self-centered darkness, these people shine as light! They raise children in a loving environment, care for the mentally handicapped and elderly, share their financial resources, and demonstrate self-sacrificing love in a myriad of ways. This is a bright light in a dark world, and people living in darkness sit up and take notice. They can't help but imagine what the world would be like if everyone had this power and lived like this."

Nick was silent for a moment before responding slowly. "That's how I felt when I watched how your church cared for Teresa. But, Andy, this is what confuses me. I meet people all the time who act as if the only thing that matters is signing some tract, standing up at some meeting, or praying some little prayer. And then if they can get you into their church, they immediately want your money. It seems like they've always just built a gymnasium or something, and now they're on the search for more people to fund it."

Andy sighed and nodded. "I had the same frustration in my search for truth. I'm not saying there is anything wrong with owning a building, but that is actually why our church on Fifth Street has chosen to rent a facility rather than put a lot of energy and money into a building."

"But if Christianity is true, then why is there so much hypocrisy? Why so many people like my mother who profess one thing while secretly living the opposite? And why all the bickering and differing opinions?"

"Excellent questions, Nick. But don't let those questions keep you from searching for truth. When I was searching, Christianity reminded me of a wide, muddy river. The people in the river were hollering at people on the bank, encouraging them to jump in and join the church. But the people on the bank looked at the muddy lives of those in the water and weren't sure. They saw hypocrisy. If the Gospel wasn't powerful enough to change people's lives, why should they jump? I struggled with that question when first looking at religions."

"So what did you do?"

"I decided to investigate further upstream. I went back to the Bible and the writings of the early church in the first two hundred years or so after Christ. Much that is being taught today would not have been recognized by those first believers as the Gospel of Jesus Christ. But if you're willing to search, you can find good, solid answers to your questions, even the ones you haven't asked yet. The Bible is an amazing book!"

Andy pointed to the Bible on his desk. "Every complaint I have ever heard about God—all his apparent injustices, the fact that he doesn't always respond when we want him to, how life seems unfair at times—all of this is in the Bible itself. Imagine the honesty of that! If I were going to write a book about an imaginary god, I certainly wouldn't include what I didn't like about him!"

Nick shoved his hands into his pockets and studied the tops of his shoes. "But if I decided to be a Christian, I would probably need to give up partying and drinking, right?"

Andy got up and walked across the room before turning toward Nick. "That is a good question, Nick, and it is true that following Jesus is costly. But it is not the most important question for you now."

"What do you mean? It's easy for you to say those things aren't important. But they are what

I live for! What is the big question I should be asking?"

Andy paused a moment before responding. "Nick, I encourage you to keep seeking God. And the question you should focus on right now is this: *Is Jesus Christ who he said he is?* And when you answer that question, answers to other questions will become clear."

Nick turned away, lost in thought. He had some serious thinking to do.

THE AUTHOR'S JOURNEY

ALTHOUGH THE CHARACTERS in this story are fictitious, the doubts expressed by Nick are not. Many people who are honestly seeking truth are asking similar questions. All of us are aware that things are not right in our world. An inner voice tells us something is seriously wrong, and we find ourselves asking questions like, *Why can't people get along? Why are human relationships so difficult? Why does poverty still exist?* Governments and aid organizations have poured billions of dollars into humanitarian aid, yet hunger continues. And what about politics? I have heard people ask why modern, educated, democratic nations can't even come up with good candidates at election time.

In light of all the scientific advances man has made, why do we still have ethnic cleansings, cruel dictators, school bullying, and mass shootings? Why do a few have so much wealth and the masses so little? Are we really able to map human DNA, travel in space, and produce a vast array of amazing electronic gadgets, yet still not feed all the children?

These things trouble us. Surely things could be better. All the pain and inequalities we see should not exist. This leads us to the question Nick struggled with: How can anyone believe that God is all-powerful and good if he's in control of this mess?

I don't know if you have struggled with this question or not, but I have. I was raised in a Christian home and taught that the Bible is truth. And yet, deep down inside, I wrestled with many questions. Where did this world come from? Is it possible, in spite of what the Bible teaches, that our universe came into being by some cosmic collision? Could it be that my existence is just the result of some freak molecular accident?

Or if, as the Bible teaches, God actually exists, how could he be loving and still allow evil to wreak havoc? As a young man this perplexed me.

Today I look at this question from a different perspective. My work takes me to impoverished developing countries, and I spend time with people who live in abject poverty. I work with children being raised in deplorable circumstances. Many live in a cycle of poverty that seems almost impossible to reverse. There are open sewers, no clean water, and little hope of meaningful change. Disease, famine, and natural disasters plague them constantly. How can a loving God see all this and allow it to continue? Doesn't he care about human misery?

I have wrestled with all these questions, yet have chosen to believe. I have come to trust in a loving God who is all-powerful. That doesn't mean this path to faith has been easy.

As I have searched for a logical answer to the question of origin, I have found evolution to be woefully inadequate. If evolution is powerful and miraculous enough to convert pond scum into the incredible complexity of life we observe around us, by now it should have easily resolved lesser issues like world poverty, human relationships, or harsh dictators. Those are simple issues compared to developing something as complex as the human eye. And further, evolution never even attempts to answer the larger question of where that original pond came from? Who put it there?

Why don't we hear more regarding this real and critical question of origin? The answer seems obvious and points to a reality that many don't want to discuss. As I observe the complexity of this amazing world we live in, I cannot escape seeing evidence for a Designer. If there is an effect, there must first be a cause.

I also have come to believe that this Ultimate Designer loves humanity. And while I am not a scientist, I have used the scientific method to come to this conclusion. My choice to believe is based on observation. Let me share what I have observed.

From childhood I have been surrounded by individuals who profess to be followers of Jesus Christ. Church life for me has been very similar to what Andy and Teresa experienced with the little group on Fifth Street. I have seen huge financial bills paid anonymously, groups of young people singing to those who are suffering, and people finding gifts of food in their kitchens. I have experienced free assistance on home improvement projects, felt an arm around my shoulder while dealing with extreme disappointment, and found nameless envelopes stuffed with cash during difficult times. These people are not perfect, but they really want to be like Jesus Christ. They see the teachings of Jesus not simply as hard sayings intended to show us how bad we are, but as God's original intent for our world. God wants us to love, share, and care for each other. He desires a world where people are concerned about the hurting, and his church today is to be a demonstration of his desires for the world. If our entire world were like the people I have been surrounded with, it would be a beautiful place.

I have seen changed lives. I have watched selfish men and women place their faith in Jesus Christ and become totally transformed. I have seen this locally, but also in many places around the globe. I think about a husband and wife in Bangladesh who recently found Jesus. In their community she had a reputation as an obnoxious, quarrelsome woman. She came to faith in Jesus, and a few months later her husband began inquiring. This couple lives in an area where believing in Jesus means risking martyrdom, so people wondered why he would choose to become a Christian.

His response was simple: "Before my wife decided to follow this Jesus, she was selfish and difficult to get along with. Now she is loving and completely changed. I have looked at my life, and I am very self-centered and can be hard to get along with. I just want this Jesus who made such a drastic change in her life to be in my life as well!"

He simply saw something powerful enough to transform, and he wanted it so badly he was willing to risk persecution. This is why I have come to love the Bible, the message of salvation through Jesus Christ, and the power he provides to those who believe.

These are just a few examples of things I have observed in the lives of those who have chosen to follow Jesus in daily life. There are still many things I don't understand. Yet I have seen enough to know that God is at work in our world, and, as the Bible tells us, God will make things right in the end.

Several years ago I was riding a bus through the city of Manila in the Philippines. Manila has one of the densest populations in the world, and a large portion of the city is a slum. The traffic crawled, and it took most of the day to get to my destination. So for hours I sat looking out at extreme poverty slowly passing by the window: rusty tin shacks, dirty half-clad children, domestic violence, and horrendous living conditions. After a couple hours of this, I suddenly became aware that I had tears running down my cheeks. This was so terribly wrong! Why is so much of the world like this?

As I wiped the tears, another profound question struck me: Why does this bother me? What is it that tells me there is a problem with this picture? If we are just cosmic accidents, freaks of some explosion, why does pain and suffering in fellow humans concern us? If there is no Creator, no absolute standard of right and wrong, and no ultimate truth, why are we troubled?

The answer was both obvious and comforting. Compassion for others spoke to me, not of some strange cosmic coincidence, but of being created by a compassionate Creator. Internal empathy reminds me that I am more than the result of colliding molecules. The Bible tells us that God created us in his image. And I found great comfort in realizing that if creation isn't content with how things are, it's because of a Creator who isn't either.

Yet I want to be very clear. Though I have chosen to believe in and follow God, I still have many questions, and there are many things I don't understand. I have lived close to people who have endured chronic pain for many years. I don't understand why God doesn't just heal them. I don't know why bad things happen to good people. I don't understand why some extremely poor countries repeatedly get hit with hurricanes, tsunamis, and crop failure. Nor do I understand why God created pleasure or why he is so extravagant with sunsets.

I can't comprehend why God has allowed the face of Christianity to become so marred—why he allows professing Christians to bear his name and claim they are following a loving Jesus while promoting violence, bombing, and military aggression. How can people claim to follow Jesus without following him?

But I also see things that give me great hope. Things that increase my faith in God. I have observed blessing coming from suffering. I have seen God work redemptively in situations that looked like tragedies. I have seen many followers of Jesus choose to live in extremely difficult and dangerous places around the globe in order to help others. The power of Jesus Christ within has empowered them to walk away from safe, middle-class America, motivated by a desire to bless the less fortunate. I have watched believers here in the United States bring aged parents into their homes during their final years, knowing that caring for them will greatly curtail their personal liberties and social lives. The list could go on.

In short, I have seen God working in the lives of others and felt his love and power transforming mine. And I have observed and experienced enough of His redemptive power to trust Him for what I cannot understand. Some situations still seem so wrong, but I live in confidence that the Bible is true. And a day is coming when all these wrongs will be made right, when evil will be overcome by good, and when those who follow Jesus now will live forever with him in peace.

There are still many things I don't understand. But I have seen enough that in spite of my questions, I have become one who openly proclaims, "God is good!"

If you have questions or would like to locate other followers of Jesus who are serious about doing what he says, please contact kingdomquestions@gmail.com.

If you would like to learn more about the kingdom of God or Christian apologetics, here are some additional resources you may want to consider:

The Kingdom That Turned the World Upside Down, *David Bercot*

This is an excellent work on the early church, her love for the kingdom of God, and how her devotion to Jesus impacted the Roman world. If you are serious about seeking God and learning about the early church, this is an excellent resource.

The Case for Faith, *Lee Strobel*

This book is written by a skeptic who decided to investigate the Christian religion for himself. The book chronicles his investigation. It is a good book for the intellectual, the doubter, and the inquisitive skeptic who seriously wants to discover the truth.

Who Moved the Stone? *Frank Morrison*

Written almost as a confession, this book was authored by a man whose purpose was to expose the Christian religion as fraudulent. He went about to prove that the resurrection of Jesus never actually occurred. But his investigation uncovered so many irrefutable historical facts that he ultimately came to faith in Jesus Christ.

Evidence That Demands a Verdict, *Josh McDowell*

Written as a reference source for serious seekers, this book contains an abundance of historical evidence substantiating the resurrection of Jesus Christ. The book provides many secular references outside of the Biblical account which support the historical accuracy of the Scriptures.

ABOUT THE AUTHOR

Gary Miller was raised in California and today lives with his wife Patty and family in the Pacific Northwest. Gary works with the poor in developing countries and directs the SALT Microfinance Solutions program for Christian Aid Ministries. This program offers business and spiritual teaching to those living in chronic poverty, provides small loans, sets up local village savings groups, and assists them in learning how to use their God-given resources to become sustainable.

ADDITIONAL RESOURCES BY GARY MILLER

BOOKS

Kingdom-Focused Finances for the Family

This first book in the Kingdom-Focused Living series is realistic, humorous, and serious about getting us to become stewards instead of owners.

Charting a Course in Your Youth

A serious call to youth to examine their faith, focus, and finances. Second book in Kingdom-Focused Living series.

Going Till You're Gone

A plea for godly examples—for older men and women who will demonstrate a kingdom-focused vision all the way to the finish line. Third book in Kingdom-Focused Living series.

The Other Side of the Wall

Stresses Biblical principles that apply to all Christians who want to reflect God's heart in giving. Applying these principles has the potential to change lives—first our own, and then the people God calls us to share with. Fourth book in Kingdom-Focused Living series.

It's Not Your Business

How involved in business should followers of Jesus be? Did God intend the workplace to play a prominent role in building his kingdom? Explore the benefits and dangers in business. Fifth and final book in the Kingdom-Focused Living series.

Budgeting Made Simple

A budgeting workbook in a ring binder; complements *Kingdom-Focused Finances for the Family*.

What Happened to Our Money?

Ignorance of Biblical money management can set young people on a path of financial hardship that results in anxiety, marital discord, depression, and envy. This short book presents foundational truths on which young couples can build their financial lives.

Life in a Global Village

Would your worldview change if the world population were shrunk to a village of one hundred people and you lived in that village? Full-color book.

This Side of the Global Wall

Pictures and graphs in this full-color book portray the unprecedented opportunities Americans have today. What are we doing with the resources God has given us?

Small Business Handbook

A manual used in microfinance programs in developing countries. Includes devotionals and practical business teaching. Ideal for missions and churches.

Following Jesus in Everyday Life

A teaching manual ideal for mission settings. Each lesson addresses a Biblical principle and includes a story and discussion questions. Black and white illustrations.

A Good Soldier of Jesus Christ

A teaching manual like *Following Jesus in Everyday Life*, but targeting youth.

Know Before You Go

Every year, thousands of Americans travel to distant countries to help the needy. But could some of these short-term mission trips be doing more harm than good? This book encourages us to reexamine our goals and methods, and prepares people to effectively interact with other cultures in short-term missions.

Jesus Really Said That?

This book presents five teachings of Jesus that are often missed, ignored, or rejected. It tells the story of Jeremy and Alicia, a couple who thought they understood Christianity and knew what it meant to be a Christian . . . until they began to look at what Jesus actually said!

Radical Islam

From the barbarous actions of ISIS to the shocking tactics of Al-Qaida, radical Islamic extremists seem to be everywhere and growing stronger. Many wonder in alarm if the movement will overtake the West and change Americans' way of life forever. How should Christians respond to this threat? Does the Bible have answers? How would Jesus respond?

AUDIO BOOKS

Kingdom-Focused Finances for the Family
Charting a Course in Your Youth
Going Till You're Gone
The Other Side of the Wall
It's Not Your Business
Life in a Global Village

SEMINARS

Kingdom-Focused Finances—Audio
This three-session seminar takes you beyond our culture's view of money and possessions, and challenges you to examine your heart by looking at your treasure. Three CDs.

Kingdom-Focused Finances—Audio and Visual
Follow along on the slides Gary uses in his seminars while you listen to the presentation. A good tool for group study or individual use. A computer is needed to view these three CDs.